EVERY FUNDRAISER

Understanding the Courage to Ask and the Factors That Drive Financial Support

OLOJO CHRISTIANA

Copyright © 2024 Olojo Christiana

All rights reserved.

ISBN: 9798302601902

INTRODUCTION

The art of fundraising stands out as the most important lifeline to the entrepreneur, nonprofit organizations, and visionaries. "**EVERY FUNDRAISER**: *Understanding the Courage to Ask & The Factors that Drive Financial Support*" invites you on a journey of transformation-a journey which transcends the mere asking of money into the heart of that which inspires, connects, and mobilizes resources for a greater purpose.

Picture yourself standing in front of a room full of potential supporters, your heart pounding as you prepare to share your vision. The stakes are high and the fear of rejection monumental. Yet, within that moment lies an unparalleled opportunity-just not to raise funding, but to fire passion, build relationships, and create a community of advocates in your mission. This book will help you develop the courage to ask, the strategies to engage, and the insight to understand what really drives financial support.

Fundraising at its core is telling stories. It's weaving a story in people's hearts and minds. That means painting a vision impressive enough to get others on that journey with you. Now, what are the specific key catalysts which can then change that simple ask into an engaging call for action? What reaches inside of people and prompts them to open their wallets to invest in your dream?

In "EVERY FUNDRAISER," we will explore these questions and more. You'll learn about the psychological underpinnings of donor motivations, the importance of authenticity in building relationships, and the art of crafting narratives that captivate and inspire. You will learn how to leverage your networks, harness the power of technology, and create a fundraising strategy that not only meets your financial goals but also fosters lasting connections.

This is not a book for the seasoned fundraiser alone, but for anyone with a vision: entrepreneurs building startups, nonprofit leaders looking to make a difference, and investors seeking opportunity with meaning. Whether you're stepping into the fundraising arena for the first time or looking to refine your approach, you'll find inestimable insights and practical strategies that empower you to embrace the courage to ask.

As you flip through the book, be prepared to change your perceptions, face what you fear, and unlock the potential within. Fundraising is not a transaction; it is a deep exchange of trust, belief, and shared purpose. Let's take this journey together to appreciate what motivates financial support for your endeavor and find the courage to ask for that which you truly need.

Welcome to "EVERY FUNDRAISER." Welcome to your journey to confident and effective fundraiser..

CONTENTS

INTRODUCTION

ACKNOWLEDGMENTS

CHAPTER 1: ---THE VISIONARY IDEA

CHAPTER 2: ------------------------BUILDING A SOLID BUSINESS PLAN

CHAPTER 3: ----------------------UNDERSTANDING YOUR AUDIENCE

CHAPTER 4: ------------------------------THE POWER OF NETWORKING

CHAPTER 5: -----------------------------CRAFTING A COMPELLING PITCH

CHAPTER 6: -------------------------------DEMONSTRATING TRACTION

CHAPTER 7: ------------------------CONFIDENCE AND AUTHENTICITY

CHAPTER 8: -------------HANDLING OBJECTIONS AND REJECTIONS

CHAPTER 9: --------------------------THE IMPORTANCE OF FOLLOW-UP

CHAPTER 10: -------------------------------LEVERAGING SOCIAL PROOF

CHAPTER 11: ----------UTILIZING TECHNOLOGY AND PLATFORMS

CHAPTER 12: ----------------------------CULTIVATING A STRONG TEAM

CHAPTER 13:----------------------NAVIGATING LEGAL AND FINANCIAL CONSIDERATIONS

CHAPTER 14:----------------------CELEBRATING SUCCESS AND LEARNING FROM FAILURE

CHAPTER 15: -----------------------THE JOURNEY BEYOND FUNDING

READERS REVIEW ON BOOK:-----SHARE YOUR THOUGHTS

ABOUT THE AUTHOR

ACKNOWLEDGMENTS

I would like to extend my heartfelt gratitude to all those who have supported me throughout the journey of writing **"EVERY FUNDRAISER**: *Understanding the Courage to Ask & The Factors that Drive Financial Support"*

First and foremost, thank you to my family and friends for your unwavering encouragement and belief in my vision. Your support has been my anchor during this endeavor.

I am deeply grateful to my mentors and colleagues who generously shared their insights and experiences, helping me to navigate the complexities of fundraising. Your wisdom has been invaluable in shaping the content of this book.

To the many fundraisers, nonprofit leaders, and supporters who shared their stories with me, thank you for your openness and willingness to contribute. Your experiences have enriched this work and provided essential lessons for readers.

I also want to acknowledge the publishing team whose expertise and dedication have brought this project to fruition.

Finally, to the readers, thank you for your interest in this journey. I hope this book inspires you to embrace the courage to ask and to forge meaningful connections that drive financial support.

Olojo Christiana.

CHAPTER 1
THE VISIONARY IDEA

It usually starts with one spark: a vision that can ignite passion, lead to action, and eventually unlock finance. This chapter examines two important aspects of creating an attractive vision and matching that vision with the market's needs as a precursor to effective fundraising.

Crafting a Compelling Vision

At the heart of every successful fundraising campaign lies a strong, compelling vision. This is the foundation upon which all fundraising efforts are built. It's not just a statement of purpose; it's a vivid picture of what could be-a future that inspires and motivates others to join in the cause.

The Power of a Strong Idea

A big idea can really connect with your potential supporters on a deep level. It clearly states a problem and an innovative, impactful solution to that problem. When developing your vision, consider the following components:

1. Clarity

It must be an easily understandable vision, not requiring a person's jargon-surfing to comprehend complicated words; the language shall be straightforward and simple using powerful words. A no-nonsense, clearly described vision gives possible supporters an effective insight into the nature of one's cause.

2. Emotion

A compelling vision evokes emotion. It should tell a story to your audience's hearts. Use anecdotes, testimonials, or word imagery to paint the picture of the difference your work is making. The more emotionally people are tied to your cause, the more they are likely to contribute.

3. Inspiration

It should inspire action-a challenge for people not to think of themselves but of the impact their support can make in the general sense. A visionary idea paints a picture of a better future and urges supporters to be part of the change.

4. Feasibility

While it is good to dream big, your vision should also be realistic. It needs to be achievable, and you must be able to show how you can achieve it. A balance between aspiration and practicality will go a long way in earning the credibility and trust of any potential donors.

The Foundation for Attracting Funds

A powerful vision, like any other powerful story, draws attention to it; on the other hand, this very attention draws into itself financial support. Clearly seeing an inspiring vision, donors become eager to invest their resources because one desires to be part of something significant-that is, such a cause that corresponds to values and aspirations.

Besides, a strong vision separates your cause from everyone else's. Amid all the noise surrounding fundraising, one clear, compelling idea will help people remember your cause. The idea is going to develop a story that can be shared with a supporter in support and builds in them the feeling of being part of something much bigger than them.

Aligning with Market Needs

While creating a strong vision is paramount, there is a greater need for your idea to rhyme with the current market trends and needs. Fundraising changes with the social dynamics, economic circumstances, and forthcoming technologies. In this light, your vision needs to comply with such dynamics.

Understanding Market Trends

To begin the process of aligning your vision to market needs, take time to conduct your research. Understand what current trends are in your sector, including:

1. Donor Preferences

What do donors currently prefer? Are they more interested in supporting a local initiative or is the interest in global causes? Understanding donor motivations can assist in crafting a vision that caters to these expectations.

2. Social Issues

What are the current trending social issues? Are there causes coming of age with the public? Anchoring your vision into current social issues will help position your vision in relevance and immediacy.

3. Technological Advances

How does technology affect fundraising? Are new platforms or tools that would serve to better reach your audience? Technology can really magnify your message and expand your reach.

Making Sure It Resonates

When you are sure what the market trends are, work your way so that your vision coincides with them. The process involves:

1. Branding Your Message

The messaging should fit into current trends and interests of donors. Describe how your vision addresses contemporary concerns and appeals to the values and aspirations of the target audience.

2. Engaging Stakeholders

Engage key stakeholders in the development of your vision, including prospective donors, community leaders, and beneficiaries. Their insight refines your idea and makes sure that the market need is appropriately met.

3. Be Flexible

Be prepared for your vision to evolve based on changes in the marketplace. One of the hallmarks of a successful fundraiser is being able to pivot and adjust as feedback and emerging trends surface.

The vision behind the idea is the key to successful fundraising. In building a clear, emotive, and inspirational vision, you provide the foundation to attract resources. Also, in developing your vision in tune with present market needs, you make it meaningful for prospective donors.

As you get into your fundraising, remember: a strong idea is not about what you want to achieve, but rather how you can inspire others to join you in that vision.

CHAPTER 2
BUILDING A SOLID BUSINESS PLAN

Any fundraising program requires a well-articulated business plan. It's like a route map that describes a vision and strategies to achieve your objectives. This chapter identifies what should be in an effective business plan and the clarity and conciseness of communicating an idea to potential investors.

Key Components of an Effective Plan

Writing a business plan requires the inclusions of some specific elements that capture the interest of investors. These components not only give full insight into your initiative but also your preparedness for success. Here are the essential elements investors look for:

1. Executive Summary

The executive summary will be the first impression investors will have of your plan. It needs to give a concise overview of your vision, mission, and the highlights of your business plan. This section should encapsulate the essence of your initiative and entice investors to read further. A compelling executive summary would include:

- A brief description of your organization and its purpose.
- The problem your initiative addresses and the solution you propose.
- Key financial projections and funding requirements.
- Summary of your target market and competitive advantage.

2. Mission and Vision Statements

Clearly written mission and vision statements bring your initiative into focus. Your mission statement must articulate the purpose and the core values of your organization, while the vision statement indicates the aspiration over the long-term. Together, they will enable an investor to get an idea of what really motivates your efforts and the change you want to effect.

3. Market Analysis

A good market analysis is indicative of your understanding of the landscape in which you are operating. This should include:

- An overview of the industry and market trends.
- Identification of your target audience and their needs.
- An analysis of competitors and your unique value proposition.

The investors want to make sure that you have researched the market and understand the dynamics that will affect the success of your initiative.

4. Marketing and Outreach Strategy

Marketing and outreach strategy describes how to achieve this support and get those dollars coming in. This could focus on brand and messaging; channels, such as through social media, events, partnerships, along with specific strategies for donor relationship development, including stewardship. Thus, an articulated strategy holds important relevance since it gives room to assured investors that you have developed strategies with much attention for awareness and eventual building up of support for this cause.

5. Operational plan

The operational plan details how your organization will function day-to-day. It should cover:

- Organizational structure and key personnel.
- How the services or programs will be delivered.
- Timeline for implementation and milestones.

Investors love an explicit operational plan because it reveals an ability to implement your vision into practice.

6. Financial Projections

Financial projections are critical in attracting funding. This section should include:

- Detailed budgets outlining expected expenses and revenue streams.
- Cash flow projections to illustrate your financial sustainability.
- Break-even analysis to show when you expect to become profitable.

Investors will scrutinize your financial projections, so it is important to provide realistic and well-supported estimates.

7. Funding Requirements

Clearly outline your funding needs and how you plan to use the funds. This section needs to spell out the following:

- The total amount of funding being sought.
- A breakdown as to how the funds will be applied, such as program costs, marketing, operational expenses.
- Possible return on investment for donors.

Being transparent about your funding needs instills confidence and thus builds trust in potential investors.

Clarity and Conciseness Matter

While what you say in your business plan is important, equally important is how you say it. Much can be done to enhance investor confidence and your chances of getting funded by being clear and concise.

Clear Communications of Your Plan

1. Use Simple Language

Avoid jargon and overly technical terms. Use straightforward language that can be easily understood by individuals who may not be familiar with your field. The essence of clear communication is that it makes access to your ideas available to a larger number of people.

2. Organize Your Content

Organize your business plan in a logical manner, using clear headings and subheadings to make it easier for readers to find their way through your plan without frustration.

3. Visual Aids

Incorporate charts, graphs, and visuals to illustrate key points. Visual aids will be able to help convey complex information more effectively and make your plan more engaging. They also break up large blocks of text, making the document easier to read.

The Importance of Conciseness

1. Be Direct

Cut to the chase. Many investors have very little time, so it is crucial to get your ideas across as briefly as possible. Avoid using too much fluff and focus on the most critical areas of your plan.

2. Keep it Short

The business plan should be as comprehensive but as short as possible. A very long plan will certainly bore the reader. Try to keep your document within reasonable length while ensuring that all essential information is included.

3. Edit Ruthlessly

After drafting your plan, take the time to review and edit it thoroughly. Remove redundant phrases, clarify ambiguous statements, and ensure that every word serves a purpose. A polished, concise document reflects professionalism and attention to detail.

Building a solid business plan is a vital step in the fundraising process. By including key components that investors look for—such as an executive summary, market analysis, and financial projections—you create a comprehensive roadmap for your initiative. Additionally, prioritizing clarity and conciseness in your communication enhances investor confidence and increases your chances of securing the necessary support.

As you embark on your journey of fundraising, remember that a well-crafted business plan will serve as a tool not only to attract funds, but also as an internal guiding document to help keep you focused on your mission and goals.

CHAPTER 3

UNDERSTANDING YOUR AUDIENCE

Knowing your audience is key to successful fundraising, which largely depends on your ability to identify possible investors and develop a strategy to appeal to their interests and motivations. This chapter shall explore the relevance of researching appropriate funding sources and targeting them, coupled with the art of adapting the pitches to investor interests.

Identifying Potential Investors

The first step in understanding your audience is the identification of potential investors who share your mission and vision. This process requires in-depth research and strategic targeting to ensure that you are reaching out to the right people or organizations likely to support your cause.

Researching Funding Sources

To effectively identify potential investors, start by doing thorough research. Here are some strategies to guide your efforts:

- *Network Analysis:* with your current network. Think about friends, family, colleagues, and acquaintances that might have an interest in your cause or contacts with potential donors. Personal relationships can often yield effective funding opportunities.

- *Foundations and Grants:* Most foundations and organizations have grants for certain causes. Research the foundation that fits your mission and check out their funding priorities. Websites like Foundation Center or GrantWatch will be of great importance in finding the available grants.

- *Identify Corporate Sponsors:* Many companies have philanthropic campaigns wherein they may be willing to sponsor programs that offer specific alignment with their corporate CSR objectives. Research companies who have a history of giving in your area and explore possibilities of partnership.

- *Identify online means:* The best online source might be crowdfunding sites or various social media. Through sources such as GoFundMe, Kickstarter, or Indiegogo, you are targeting people who want to give, who have the desire and, moreover, potential passion about supporting an innovative idea. Social media will help one identify influential persons and advocate business lines.
- *Networking Events:* Industry conferences, workshops, and networking events are great places to meet potential investors in person. Such gatherings provide opportunities to build relationships and share your vision with individuals who may be interested in supporting your cause.

Targeting the Right Investors

After having identified prospective sources of funding, the next important thing is targeting the right investors. This will involve studying their interests, values, and giving history to identify whether they will be appropriate for your initiative. Consider the following:

- *Mission Alignment*: Determine whether the would-be investor's values are in line with your mission. The likelihood of an investor supporting a cause is when it speaks to their personal beliefs or corporate objectives.

- *Giving History:* Research the giving history of the prospective investors. Try to find a pattern in their past contributions regarding the kind of organizations they have supported and the amounts they have donated. This will help in knowing their funding priorities.

- *Engagement Level:* Consider the level of engagement potential investors have with your cause. Are they already supporters, or have they shown interest in similar initiatives? Engaged investors are more likely to contribute and advocate for your cause.

Tailoring Your Approach

After identifying and targeting potential investors, a critical next step involves adjusting your approach. Customization of pitches to meet the investors' interests goes a great way in enhancing the probability of raising finances.

Understanding Investor Motivations

The first important thing when customizing your approach involves grasping what motivates those investors that you are prospecting. Common motivations will generally include:

- *Passion for the Cause:* Most investors are motivated by a genuine passion for the issues your organization addresses. Knowing this will help you frame your pitch in a manner that speaks to their values.

- ***Desire for Impact:*** Investors often look at ways in which they can make a meaningful impact with their contributions. Highlighting tangible outcomes of their support can be a great motivator.
- ***Tax Benefits:*** Some of them will be motivated by the tax benefits that come along with giving to a charity. Presenting the information on tax deductions may be an attractive feature of your pitch.
- ***Reputation and Recognition:*** To some corporate sponsors, the support of a cause is a means to improve their brand reputation. The emphasis on the visibility and recognition they will get could be an effective way of engaging such investors.

Personalizing Your Pitches

Knowing clearly why investors invest will help you tailor your pitches to their motives. Following are a few tips that you may want to consider:

- ***Personalize Your Message:*** Keep in mind the unique interests and values of each investor. Make sure you use his or her name, refer to his or her past contributions, and demonstrate how your initiative is part of his or her philanthropic goals.
- ***Focus on Impact:*** Clearly articulate the impact of their support. Using data, stories, and testimonials will help to paint a picture of how their contributions will make a difference. Investors want to be shown what tangible outcomes their investment will yield.
- ***Address Concerns:*** Anticipate what concerns or objections investors might have and proactively address them in your pitch. This shows that you have thought through the challenges and are prepared to navigate them.

Offer Avenues of Engagement

Provide donors with opportunities to engage with your organization beyond the dollar investment. This might include event invites, volunteer activities, or regular communications of impact because of their support. In this way, investors are engaged and will own a commitment to your cause.

Understanding your audience is a key ingredient in successful fundraising. Through research in identifying potential investors and targeting the right sources of funding, you successfully pave the way toward proper connections. Besides, your approach tailored to interest fits your best chances of support.

As you move on with your journey in fundraising, remember that building the relationship with the probable investors is as important as making the ask.

CHAPTER 4
THE POWER OF NETWORKING

It is again proven by the saying "it's not what you know but who you know." Networking opens the path to funding opportunities and makes a set of meaningful relationships that go beyond financial support. In this chapter, we would look upon how to build relationships using networking and how the connections which are already available with someone could be used to get an introduction to potential investors.

Building Meaningful Relationships

In fact, networking is essentially relationship-building. Relationships not based on transactions, but based on the values aligned, mutual respect, and trust. Such meaningful relationships in fundraising can bring forth opportunities otherwise not realized.

Role of Networking and the Creation of Funding Opportunities

Networking plays an integral role in the realm of fundraising in several important respects:

Access to Resources
Networking will further present you with people who have access to resources, which include money, expertise, and advice. These contacts can present an opportunity to gain insight on ways to go about raising money or problems that one may come across.

- *Building Trust:* Relationships formed through networking build trust. Potential investors are more likely to grant you money for your initiatives if they know you on a personal level and can see your commitment to your cause. Trust forms the foundation for donations or financial contributions.

- *Creating Advocates:* Networking can turn acquaintances into advocates. When people believe in your mission and have a personal connection to you, they are more likely to champion your cause within their own networks. This can bring new funding opportunities and increased visibility for your organization.

- *Learning from Others:* Through networking, one gets to an opportunity to learn from others who are successful in the fundraising lot. The interaction with experienced fundraisers will provide valuable insight, strategies, and best practices that can be used in enhancing your own efforts.

Strategies for Effective Networking
To power networking, the following strategies should be considered.

- *Attend Events:* Industry conferences, workshops, and networking events are an ideal platform to present your cause before a host of people. Meet the potential investors, collaborators, and mentors, but don't forget to have your elevator pitch ready. Join Professional Associations: The memberships of professional associations that come under the ambit of your cause could help in networking. Many such associations often have events, resources, and means of connecting members.

Social Media Engagement

Leverage LinkedIn, Twitter, and Facebook to build up a network of acquaintances within your industry. Post content related to your brand and chime in whenever relevant to start building relationships for later pitching to investors or business collaborators. Social media might be the most powerful tool for one desiring to build relationships with ease.

Follow Up

When you meet someone in an event or through other persons, you should do a follow-up with them by sending personalized messages. Let them know that you enjoyed the talk and would want to stay connected. Continued follow-through helps solidify relationships and keeps you on their radar.

Leveraging Existing Connections

After building your network, it's time to leverage the people you already know to introduce you to investors. Your current relationships can be the best in helping you reach out to a new circle and attracting potential funding.

Utilizing Your Network

Following are some of the strategies to be able to effectively leverage your existing network:

- *Identify Key Contacts:* Look through your network for people who might have relationships with potential investors. That could be friends, colleagues, mentors, or acquaintances who have highly connected networks in your industry.

    Request Introductions: Do not hesitate to contact your network and ask for introductions to anyone they may know that might fit into your cause. Be specific about whom you'd like to be introduced to and why. In this way, it clearly defines how the contact can best facilitate an introduction.

- *Offer Value:* Whenever asking for introductions, be clear about how you might reciprocate value with contacts. This can be sharing insight and helping their initiatives move along or even connecting them to contacts in your network. In building reciprocal relationships, your network will strengthen and others will support your fundraising efforts.

- *Utilize Alumni Networks:* If you went to a university or college, leverage your alumni network. Many institutions have alumni associations that make such networking among graduates easier. Many alumni feel a sense of loyalty to their alma mater and may be more inclined to support initiatives associated with it.

Relationship Building

As you use your network, it's important to develop the relationships over time. Here are a few tips that will help you nurture and grow your network:

- *Stay Engaged:* Keep in regular contact with your contacts, even if you don't have a specific request. Share updates about your initiatives, ask about their projects, and show genuine interest in their work. Staying engaged keeps the lines of communication open and fosters goodwill.
- *Updates:* Provide updates on the progress of your fundraising to your network. Be transparent with the successes, milestones reached, and how their contribution impacts. This builds trust and reinforces the network's engagement in continuous support.
- *Appreciate:* You must thank your supporters for their assistance. You can never go wrong with thank you notes or messages that you would love to have a continued relationship with, by the courtesy of their support.

Networking is not to be underestimated in the fundraising landscape. Building meaningful relationships creates a foundation for funding opportunities and fosters trust among potential investors. You can expand your reach and access new funding sources by leveraging your existing connections and nurturing those relationships.

Keep in mind, as you forge on in your journey of fundraising, it's not all about the asks; it's building up a community of people who believe in your mission.

CHAPTER 5
CRAFTING A COMPELLING PITCH

The ability to make a persuasive pitch is an essential ability in not getting financially destroyed. The successful pitch hooks not just the attention of prospective investors but goes all the way into convincing them emotionally to act. Herein, the elements which would amount to a perfect pitch, and storytelling as an extraordinary tool of persuasion will be found.

Elements of a Successful Pitch

A well-structured pitch is about communicating effectively to hold the attention of prospective investors. Following are the key elements of your pitch:

1. Introduction-easy and to the point

Introduce yourself, your organization, and the purpose of the pitch. The opening should be interesting; this is where you have to set the tone of the rest of your presentation. You want to draw in the attention of all listeners within the first few seconds of your presentation, which is where you will make your first impression.

2. Define the Problem

Clearly articulate the problem or need that your initiative seeks to address, using data, statistics, or real-life examples to illustrate the importance of the issue. This will help prospective investors understand the urgency and relevance of your cause. A well-defined problem instills a sense of necessity and forms the basis on which to present your solution.

3. Present Your Solution

Now that you have established the problem, provide the solution. Describe how your organization is poised to solve the problem and, specifically, how. The impact of your solution to the people should be spelled out, showing how your solution will make a change in their lives. You need to exude an air of confidence in this approach-when describing and showcasing your plan. There needs to be a great reason behind it.

4. Highlight Your Unique Value Proposition

Describe what sets your organization apart from other similar organizations. Define your value proposition. What makes it unique? Is it an innovative approach, expertise, or successes accomplished? When you are in a position to articulate these strengths clearly, this may give investors a reason to invest in your initiative.

5. Prove Impact

Investors want to be sure that their money will achieve something. Include any past successes your organization has had, such as metrics, testimonials, or case studies showing the impact of your work. This proof helps build credibility and gives potential investors confidence that their investment will be put to good use.

6. Describe Funding Needs

Be transparent about your funding needs: clearly state how much money you are seeking and how it will be distributed. The section includes a breakdown of expenses, and a timeline for the implementation of these funds. This gives the potential investors a clear picture of the investment scope and the purpose of its use.

7. Call to Action

Close your pitch with a solid call to action. Invite your potential investors to take the next step: a follow-up meeting, donation, or connection with others in their network. A strong and clear call to action guides and mobilizes people.

Engaging Through Storytelling

While the elements of a successful pitch are essential, the way you deliver your message can significantly impact its effectiveness. Storytelling is a powerful technique that can engage potential investors on an emotional level and make your pitch more memorable.

1. The Power of Narrative

Humans are naturally drawn to stories. A well-crafted narrative can evoke emotions, create connections, and inspire action. When you incorporate storytelling into your pitch, you transform abstract concepts into relatable experiences. Here are some techniques for using narrative to persuade investors:

2. Use Personal Stories

Personal stories can be incredibly impactful. Share anecdotes about individuals or communities who have benefited from your organization's work. These stories humanize your cause and allow potential investors to see the real-world impact of their support. Personal narratives create empathy and can motivate investors to contribute.

3. Create a Hero's Journey

Frame your pitch as a hero's journey, where your organization is the hero working to overcome challenges and make a difference. This narrative structure can help potential investors see themselves as part of the solution. Highlight the obstacles you've faced, the triumphs you've achieved, and the vision you have for the future. This approach fosters a sense of partnership and shared purpose.

4. Use Vivid Imagery

Incorporate vivid imagery into your storytelling to paint a picture in the minds of your audience. Use descriptive language to evoke emotions and create a sense of urgency. For example, instead of simply stating statistics about homelessness, describe a day in the life of an individual experiencing homelessness. This technique helps potential investors connect emotionally with your cause.

5. Incorporate Testimonials

Including testimonials from beneficiaries, volunteers, or supporters can add credibility to your narrative. These voices provide authentic perspectives on the impact of your organization's work. Testimonials can serve as powerful endorsements that reinforce the importance of your mission and the effectiveness of your approach.

6. Keep It Authentic

Authenticity is key in storytelling. Be genuine in your delivery and share both successes and challenges. Investors appreciate transparency and are more likely to connect with a narrative that feels real and relatable. Avoid overly polished or rehearsed stories; instead, focus on conveying your passion and commitment to your cause.

Crafting a compelling pitch is an essential skill for any fundraiser. By incorporating the key elements of a successful pitch and leveraging the power of storytelling, you can capture the attention and interest of potential investors.

A well-structured pitch not only conveys your message effectively but also engages your audience on an emotional level, inspiring them to take action. As you prepare to make your pitch, remember that confidence and authenticity are crucial.

CHAPTER 6
DEMONSTRATING TRACTION

Showing traction puts meaning and context into this for a potential investor-a view toward the viability and impact of your initiative. Traction is basically proof that the organization gains momentum in a meaningful manner to meet real market demand. This chapter sets out to discuss how one can prove market demand with a showing of traction and focuses on only the key metrics that are valued by those offering funding.

Proving Market Demand

Investors will most likely believe in initiatives that have an evident demand in the marketplace. The proof of demand for your solution builds credibility for the team and ensures the investors that their contribution to the cause will be productive. Here are a few strategies to demonstrate market demand effectively:

1. Conduct Market Research
Conducting proper market research is very vital in proving market demand. The research should include:

- *Identification of Target Audience:* Clearly identify who your target audience is and what specific needs your initiative addresses. Understanding your audience allows you to tailor your messaging and show that you are meeting a real demand.

- *Competitor Analysis:* Understand the competition in which your organization operates and its place within that market. Identify current solutions, pointing out how and where your solution differs. This can also help in articulating the unique value proposition of your initiative.

- *Data Collection:* Quantitative and qualitative data can be used to support your claims. Surveys, interviews, and focus groups will provide an idea about the needs and preferences of your target audience. Presenting this data in your pitch may strengthen your case for market demand.

2. Highlight Early Successes

Demonstrating traction often involves showcasing early successes that indicate market demand. Consider the following:

Pilot Programs

If you have done pilot programs or initial projects, share the results. Highlight how many participants, the feedback received, and any positive outcomes achieved. Early successes can serve as powerful testimonials to the effectiveness of your solution.

- *User Engagement:* In case of possibility, the evidence of user engagement in your product or service. Things such as the number of signed-up users, active users, and customer retention rate may help to prove a certain interest and demand for what you offer.

- *Partnerships and Collaborations:* Highlight any partnerships or collaborations with established organizations or influencers in your field. These endorsements can lend credibility to your initiative and signal to investors that there is a recognized need for your solution.

3. Leverage Testimonials and Case Studies

Testimonials and case studies can be compelling evidence of market demand. Consider the following approaches:

- *Story of Beneficiaries:* Share the story of an individual or the community that has benefited from your initiative. Personal stories help to illustrate the impact of your work and show the demand for your solution.

- *Case Studies:* Prepare case studies that outline a specific instance where your organization has successfully addressed a need. Include metrics, outcomes, and testimonials to help paint a full picture of your impact.

Key Metrics That Matter

When it comes to attracting funding, highlighting the key performance indicators is paramount. Investors would want to see what is measurable to prove that your initiative is effective and will be sustainable. Some of the key metrics one may consider include:

1. Financial Metrics

Financial metrics provide insight into the fiscal health and sustainability of your organization. The key financial indicators include:

- *Revenue Growth:* Showing consistent revenue growth over a period is good proof of market demand for your product and workability of the business model. Highlight any trends in the generation of revenue and future growth projections.

- *Profit Margins:* Where applicable, provide your profit margins as an indication of financial efficiency. Generally, investors are interested in understanding how well costs are controlled in relation to revenue.

Funding Utilization

Clearly outline how any previous funding has been used and the impact that this has had on your organization. This kind of transparency develops trust and shows you to be responsible stewards of the financial resources.

2. Impact Metrics

Impact metrics quantify the effectiveness of your initiative in accomplishing its mission. These metrics will differ depending on your organization's goals but may include:

Beneficiary Reach

Showcase the number of people or communities served by your initiative. This metric portrays the scale of your impact and the demand for your services.

- *Outcome Measures:* Use specific outcome measures that can help you in depicting the effectiveness of your solution. For example, if your organization addresses educational inequalities, you may track an improvement in test scores or graduation rates in beneficiaries.

- *Satisfaction Rates:* Collect data from beneficiaries and stakeholders regarding their satisfaction with your services. High satisfaction rates could mean that you address a very real need, and your solution is effective.

3. Engagement Metrics

Engagement metrics tell a story of the effectiveness of audience interaction with your organization. These may include:

- *User Growth:* This measures, over time, how many more users or audience members are growing. A consistent rate of growth among users signals increasing interest and demand for your undertaking.

- ***Retention Rates:*** The proportion of users or beneficiaries who remain with your organization over some time. High retention rates would show that your solution is of value to them and they feel benefited by it.

- ***Social Media Engagement:*** Number of likes, shares, comments on social media platforms. A high level of engagement will reveal a very strong connection with your audience; there might even be community building around your cause.

Demonstrating traction is key to proving market demand and unlocking funding. Show this through deep market research, early successes, and leveraging your testimonials in a strong case for your initiative. Besides, financial, impact, and engagement key metrics show investors the measurable outcomes that they look for.

Last but not least, when it comes to the delivery of your pitch, remember that traction doesn't necessarily have to be numerical; it can also be a story of overall progress and potentials.

CHAPTER 7
CONFIDENCE AND AUTHENTICITY

The most important aspects are confidence and authenticity. They not only help you express your initiative but also greatly affect the perception potential investors will have about you and your organization. This chapter discusses the importance of projecting confidence and the critical role of authenticity in building trust and securing financial support.

Confidence Projection

Confidence is perhaps the most potent tool in the fundraiser's toolkit. If you can make them feel confident, it will serve to frame investor perceptions positively and greatly enhance your chances of success. Following are some of the most salient aspects of projecting confidence effectively:

The Power of Body Language
Your body language will tell a lot about how confident you appear. Consider the following:

- *Posture:* Always stand tall and open. Never cross your arms or slouch, as that shows insecurity; rather, keep your shoulders back and head held high to exude confidence.

- *Eye Contact:* Establish eye contact with your audience; it conveys interest and confidence. It tells them you believe in your message and you are comfortable sharing it. However, be culturally sensitive about the issue of eye contact as the norm does vary.

- *Gestures:* Use purposeful gestures to emphasize key points in your pitch. Avoid fidgeting or overly nervous movements because these detract from your message. Confident gestures enhance your delivery and reinforce your commitment to your cause.

Mastering Your Message

Confidence comes from preparation. The more you know your pitch and the substance of your initiative, the more confident you will be. Following are some tips to help you own your message:

- *Practice:* Practice your pitch several times alone and in front of others. This practice will allow you to perfect your delivery, find areas to improve, and become more comfortable with your content.

- **Anticipate Questions**: Be prepared for any questions or possible objections investors may have. By anticipating these questions, you can answer them confidently and show how well you know your initiative.

- *Know Your Numbers:* Know by heart the key metrics and data that support your argument. Confidence in your numbers builds credibility and reassures investors that you are on top of your organization's performance.

Embracing Vulnerability

While projecting confidence is paramount, allowing some type of vulnerability to peek through is even more so. Sharing challenges or uncertainties makes your pitch so much more human, relatable, and real. Here's how you can get that balance:

- *Share Challenges:* If your organization has overcome some obstacles, don't be afraid to share them. Showing challenges means complete transparency, and you are prepared for any difficulty that might knock on your door.

- *Growth:* Emphasize how these situations were opportunities for growth and learning, and how you had adapted and changed in response to a setback. The approach will convey resilience and confidence in your ability to overcome future hurdles.

The Importance of Being Authentic

Authenticity is one of the cornerstones of effective fundraising. You create a bond of trust with potential investors where the atmosphere is genuine and transparent, which is important to secure investment support. Below are some key aspects of authenticity to consider:

Building Trust Through Honesty

Honesty is the foundation that lays the cement for trust. Investors want to be assured that you are honest about your mission and that their money serves a purpose. Here are ways to engender trust through honesty:

- *Be Transparent About Goals:* Clearly articulate your organization's goals and the impact you hope to create. Do not exaggerate or overpromise. Transparency about your goals helps investors understand what they are supporting.

  Acknowledge Limitations: If there are limitations to your initiative or uncertainties about the future, be upfront about them. The acknowledgment of such factors shows integrity and lets investors make their decisions with full knowledge of the facts.

- **Share Real Stories:** Use real stories of beneficiaries or stakeholders to illustrate the impact of your work. Real-life narratives, other than abstract concepts, touch the hearts of investors more and help them connect emotionally with your cause.

Stay Loyal to Your Ideals

Authenticity also means staying true to the values and mission. How to make sure that your pitch is in tune with core principles of your organization:

- **Align Your Message with Your Mission:** Make sure that your message is well-aligned with your organizational mission and values. It helps self-affirm and confirm for you your commitment to your cause and that you really are concerned with trying to make a difference.

Be yourself. It doesn't sound like it is forced. It's a part of you, and you are sharing that passion about your cause. To investors, they can better relate to you when you're real and relatable.

- **Relate to Them:** Building rapport with your investors goes beyond just making a pitch. Take the time to engage them, listen to their point of view, and understand what motivates them to support causes. The relational way helps build trust and promotes long-term partnerships.

The Power of Vulnerability

Being authentic also means embracing vulnerability. Sharing your journey of highs and lows can create a deeper connection with your audience. Here's how to leverage vulnerability effectively:

- *Share Personal Motivations:* Discuss what drives your passion for your cause. Sharing your personal connection to the mission can evoke empathy and inspire others to support your work.

- *Acknowledge the Journey:* Fundraising is a journey-up and down. Sharing experiences of setbacks and lessons learned may better resonate with some venture capital investors who value the challenges of pursuing meaningful work.

Confidence and authenticity will get you through successful fundraising. By projecting confidence in your body language, preparation, and even in vulnerable states, while being authentic and transparent, you will gain the trust and reliable contact of potential supporters.

Keep in mind that confidence and authenticity balance each other as you prepare to make your ask. Next, the courage to ask for support, including strategies that will empower you to make that ask with clarity and conviction.

CHAPTER 8
HANDLING OBJECTIONS AND REJECTIONS

Objections and rejections are inevitable. Even the most compelling pitches can encounter skepticism, and not every ask will result in a positive response. However, how you handle these challenges can significantly impact your success as a fundraiser. This chapter will explore strategies for anticipating investor concerns and effectively responding to objections, as well as how to cultivate resilience in the face of rejection.

Anticipating Investor Concerns

Being able to anticipate common objections investors will make and plan persuasive responses is a very powerful tool to avoid getting stuck in uncomfortable situations. Here are some classic concerns and ways to respond to them:

1. Financial Viability

- *Objection:* "I'm not sure your organization can sustain itself financially."

- *Response:* To alleviate concerns about financial viability, clear financial metrics and projections should be shown. Share your organization's revenue streams, funding history, and budget allocations. Highlight successful fundraising campaigns or partnerships that prove your ability to generate income. In fact, a well-structured financial plan will go a long way in reassuring the investor that indeed you have a sustainable model.

2. **Impact Measurement**

    - *Objection:* "How can I be sure that my investment will make a difference?

    - *Response:* Investors want to understand that their contribution will lead to tangible impact. To answer this, it's important to present various data and case studies that represent the impact of your organization. Highlight specific metrics around how previous funding has led to a measurable outcome. Describe your plan for ongoing measurement and reporting on impact so that investors will be assured they will get updates about the results of their investment.

3. **Competition and Market Demand**

    - *Objection:* "There are already several organizations addressing this issue. What makes you different?"

    - *Response:* Differentiate your organization by clearly articulating your unique value proposition. Highlight what sets your approach apart from competitors, whether it's your innovative methods, specialized expertise, or community engagement strategies. Use market research to demonstrate the demand for your solution and explain how your organization fills a specific gap in the landscape.

4. Leadership and Team Capability

- *Objection:* "Do you have the right team in place to execute this initiative?"

- *Response:* Investors mostly consider the leaders and the team behind the initiative. To get over this, describe the qualifications of your team members and their relevant experience. Highlight the respective background, skills, and accomplishments. If possible, include third-party testimonials or endorsements from recognized authorities that speak volumes about the confidence others instill in your team for getting the job done.

5. Timing and Commitment

- *Objection:* "I don't think this is a good time for me to invest."

- *Response:* Yes, there does come a point when the time is right in an investor's mind to decide to invest. To this effect, begin to have a discussion about priorities and challenges at the time being. Be prepared to do some follow-up correspondence for those that may be interested in later times. Sometimes nurturing this relationship over time does result in opportunities to ask for support.

Resilience in the Face of Rejection

Rejection is part of the process when fundraising, and how you respond to it may shape your future success. It is important to develop resilience in order not to lose your motivation and to learn from your setbacks. Here are some strategies to help you bounce back:

1. Reframe Rejection

Instead of treating rejection as some sort of personal failure, consider the opportunity for growth. Know that each "no" is one step closer to a "yes." Some ways to look at this would be:

- *Learning from Feedback:* If an investor rejects and gives feedback, make use of it to learn something new. Analyze what

went wrong from their perspective and see how you can work on it in your next pitches.
- ***Criticism-Seek Constructive Criticism:*** Right after rejection, ask the investor for constructive criticism-or ask some trusted colleagues. Once you understand their point of view, you are able to tune your approach and improve a future pitch.

2. Maintain a Positive Mindset

A positive mindset is at the very core of resilience. The following are techniques that shall help you build positivity in your thoughts.

- ***Practice Gratitude:*** Think about those aspects of your job you are grateful for. Such practice will make you focus more on the positive difference you create than on setbacks.

- ***Visualize Success:*** Practice visualization to see yourself succeeding. Visualize yourself presenting your case with confidence and receiving positive feedback. Such practice may inspire your confidence and motivation.

3. Build a Support Network

Having a support network around you will help you to get through the challenges of fundraising. Consider:

- ***Connect with Peers:*** Engage with fellow fundraisers or professionals in your field. Sharing experiences and challenges can provide valuable insights and encouragement.

- ***Seek Mentorship:*** Find a mentor who has experience in fundraising. Their guidance and perspective can help you navigate obstacles and maintain motivation during tough times.

4. Set Realistic Goals

Setting realistic and achievable goals can help you maintain focus and motivation. Consider the following strategies:

- ***Break Down Goals:*** Be sure to break larger, overarching goals down into their smaller, more manageable elements. This builds momentum and keeps spirits high even from the slightest achievements.

- **_Track Progress:_** Record progress pertaining to your fundraising initiatives-both successes and hurdles. Monitoring activities can provide a feeling of satisfaction for a job well done that keeps many motivated.

5. Self-Care Practices

To achieve resilience, you should show concern for both your body and mind. You may want to apply the following self-care activities:

- **_Relaxation Activities:_** Those that keep you fit and fresh, such as exercises, meditation, or hobbies, will help you stay positive in life.

- **_Reflect and Recharge:_** Give yourself time to reflect on the experiences and recharge in case of setbacks. Sometimes, taking breaks helps you return to work with energy and a fresh perspective.

The journey to fundraising is full of objections and rejections. Anticipate various investors' concerns, and prepare your quick but real responses to pass through such difficult conversations confidently. Further, resilience to rejections will help you get motivated, knowing full well that one learns even from those setbacks.

So go on, raise funds, remembering every problem is an opportunity.

CHAPTER 9
THE IMPORTANT FOLLOW-UP

Asking for money is only the beginning of a much larger process. The ask itself may be critical, but in most cases, it is the follow-up that determines whether or not that ask is successful. Follow-up is not simply a nicety; it's a strategic necessity with major implications for the sustainability of financial support. This chapter will explore the role of follow-up in fundraising, focusing on how to maintain communication and build long-term relationships.

Nurture by Communicating

Communication forms the lifeline for any fundraising effort to thrive. An initial 'ask' should be followed with equally or even more, well-placed, appropriately timed follow-ups to continue the conversation. This conversation is multidimensional in role - including to:

1. Reinforcing Connection

Second, donors require time to consider their decision after the initial ask. A timely follow-up may act to strengthen the relationship that you have built, reminding the donor of the need you represent and the difference they can make. It shows you value their support and are genuinely interested in what they think and feel about the request.

2. Additional Information

Sometimes, donors would like to ask a few questions or need more information before commitment. A follow-up can provide that opportunity to answer questions, tell success stories, or update on recent happenings within your organization. This context helps them feel all the more certain they make a good choice in selecting to support your cause.

3. Accountability

Follow-up after an ask shows accountability and professionalism. It says you are committed to transparency and that you value the donor's time and consideration. That accountability builds trust-the holy grail in any donor relationship.

4. Encouraging Engagement

A follow-up can also extend a specific invitation to engagement, such as inviting donors to events or asking them to volunteer, or their feelings, in which their closeness and connection to your organization increases. It is known that engaging your donors across various touchpoints has a positive impact on their long-term loyalty and support.

Building Long-Term Relationships

While immediate funding is great, the real objective of any fundraising effort is building a long-term relationship with donors. This requires sustained contact and engagement. Relationship-building is fostered in the following ways:

1. A sense of community

Donors will be more inclined to continue their support when they feel part of a community. You can create a sense of belonging through regular follow-ups. Sharing updates of the success stories and the impact their contributions have helps donors to find their place in your organization's mission.

2. Building Loyalty

Loyalty is developed by simply keeping in constant communication and interaction. By following up on your organization regularly, you have the ability to stay at the top of the donors' minds. The recurring relationship can lead to increasing support over time because committed donors are more likely to give again and even increase their giving.

3. Identifying New Opportunities

With long-term relationships often come further possibilities for collaboration and support. By following up regularly, one can find out whether it could be on events, campaigns, or other activities in which partnership might be built. Engaging donors in such a manner offers novel ideas and increased funding.

4. Encouraging Legacy Giving

As relationships deepen, donors may consider legacy giving or planned gifts. By keeping in contact and showing the impact of their support, you will be able to encourage donors to think about their long-term commitment to your organization. This can lead to significant financial support that extends beyond their immediate contributions.

5. Feedback and Improvement

Finally, follow-up allows for feedback. You can learn by asking your donors about experiences and perceptions, and you can use such information to improve fundraising strategies. The feedback loop will enhance not only the effectiveness of your organization but also let the donors know their opinions count, and it furthers the building of the relationship.

Follow-up in fundraising is one thing that can never be overstated. Follow-up will enable one to cultivate through follow-ups on time. It helps in building relationships, adding information, and accountability to people, thus creating more engagements.

It is about developing ongoing relationships with donors, acquiring continued support and commitment for your organization. Having follow-up as one of your base focuses in fundraising, relationships will be built that create finances for the advancement of your mission. Remember, the courage to ask is but the beginning; it is the courage to follow through that actually translates potential into lasting impact.

CHAPTER 10
LEVERAGING SOCIAL PROOF

Social proof is a pretty powerful concept that can help a lot with your credibility and impress potential investors. The psychological phenomenon of social proof involves the actions and opinions of others guiding your own behavior. In fundraising, this may be in the form of testimonials, endorsements, and building a community of support. This chapter will show how to effectively leverage social proof to bolster your fundraising efforts.

The Power of Testimonials and Endorsements

Testimonials and endorsements are strong forms of social proof that can help build your organization's credibility and encourage potential investors to invest in your cause. Here's how to effectively make use of these tools:

1. The Power of Positive Feedback

Positive feedback or testimonials from beneficiaries, partners, or any well-renowned figure in your field may go a long way in the way potential investors view your organization. Here are some key strategies for the use of testimonials:

- *Collect Real Testimonials:* Reach out to people who have been directly impacted by your work or with whom you have worked on a project. Ask them to describe their experiences and how your organization has impacted their life or community. Be authentic; people relate more to real stories than general praise.

- *Specific Outcomes:* When obtaining the testimonies, ask for specific outcomes or changes your organization's effort brought about. In other words, as opposed to general statements such as, "This is a great organization," an effective delivery of this testimonial might be: "Thank you, [Your Organization], through whom I was able to obtain the scholarship that truly changed my life.

- *Diverse Voices:* Include testimonials from multiple parties, such as beneficiaries, volunteers, donors, and community leaders. Diversity helps to add depth to your narrative and showcases the wide scope of your organization.

2. Testimonials from Influencers

Testimonials from leading names in your industry may greatly boost the credibility of your organization. Here's how to get and use such testimonials:

- *Key Influencers Identification:* Research those who are highly reputed within the industry or community. It can be any industry leader, politician at local levels, or popular advocate for any cause.

- *Build Relationships*: It is always better to build relationships with these influencers before seeking an endorsement. Interact with them through social media, attend their events, or invite them to participate in your initiatives. Building rapport increases the likelihood that they will support your cause.

- **Request Endorsements with Intention:** When soliciting for an endorsement, ensure the 'why' for needing such support is well articulated, explaining its congruence with their values or mission; provide information necessary concerning the organization and also concerning that particular project one may require it for.

- **Prominently Display Endorsements:** Once secured, showcase those endorsements prominently on your website, in your marketing materials, and fundraising pitches. Highlighting the endorsement from a reputable figure will surely enhance credibility for your organization to encourage interested investors to act now.

Creating a Community of Supporters

The core of using social proof lies in building a community of supporters. A strong network of advocates can give credence to your project, amplify your message, and create a sense of shared investment in your cause. Below are ways to build and foster such a community.

1. Engage Your Supporters
The key to developing a community of advocates is to keep them engaged. Here are ways to foster engagement:

- **Regular Communication:** Communicate your organization's activities, successes, and challenges to your supporters. Use newsletters, social media, and personal outreach to keep the lines of communication open.

- **Invite Participation:** Encourage supporters to get involved with your initiatives, whether by volunteering, attending events, or sharing your message within their networks. The more they are connected with your work, the more likely they are to become advocates for your cause.

- ***Create Opportunities for Feedback:*** Request feedback from your supporters about your initiatives and fundraising efforts. This will help you gauge what needs improvement, and they will feel valued and heard.

2. Develop a Feeling of Belonging

Developing a feeling of belonging amongst your supporters can rise their commitment to your cause. Consider the following strategies.

- ***Events Hosting:*** Organize events for your supporters, either physically or virtually. Such an event might make people relate to one another, create a feeling of being in a team, and somehow make them feel they share something in common.

- Give recognition and celebrate different contributions that your supporters pay off. Expressing appreciation might deepen their feelings for your organization, be it shout-outs on social media, acknowledgments during events, or personal thank-you notes.

- ***Share Success Stories:*** Regularly share success stories that highlight the impact of your supporters' contributions. This reinforces the idea that they are part of something meaningful and encourages them to continue advocating for your cause.

3. Empower Advocates to Share Your Message

Encouraging your supporters to share your message can amplify your reach and enhance your credibility. Here's how to empower them:

- ***Shareable Content:*** Develop interesting content that your supporters can share within their networks. This can be in the form of social media posts, infographics, videos, or success stories about the work your organization does.

- ***Encourage Personal Stories:*** Encourage supporters to share personal stories regarding your cause. Personal stories are very influential for others, and it might encourage other people to take part.

Referral Program: A referral program may thus be designed to encourage the supporters to refer potential investors to your organization. This would create a snowballing effect, expanding your network and increasing your chances of securing support.

Social proof can be a very powerful strategy in the improvement of your fundraising through the testimony and endorsements you get from the community. Good feedback about your organization builds on their credit score, which might affect huge changes in the decision-making processes of potential investors. This helps you create an outspoken group that speaks well for you and multiplies your voice and network, leading to the facilitation of finance coming your way.

As you go along on your journey in fundraising, social proof is not just about numbers, it's about the story, the relationship, and therefore the engagement to build together a difference.

CHAPTER 11
UTILIZING TECHNOLOGY AND PLATFORMS

Technology forms a broad landscape in fundraising. Better use of technology-from online crowdfunding to other digital marketing strategies-significantly helps in reaching new investors to secure financial investments. The present chapter will discuss a variety of online fundraising tools, using effective digital strategies that enable investor attraction, especially with the help of social media.

Exploring Online Fundraising Tools

Online fundraising innovations have transformed the way groups raise money. Of all fundraising options, crowdfunding has perhaps received the most attention, offering the opportunity for individuals and organizations to raise money from multiple people, often in small increments. Here's an overview of some key crowdfunding platforms and their benefits:

1. Popular Crowdfunding Platforms

- *Kickstarter:* This is mainly designed for creative projects. Kickstarter allows creators to present their ideas and set funding goals. Backers receive rewards based on their contribution levels, hence being attractive to artists, inventors, and entrepreneurs.

- *Indiegogo:* Similar to Kickstarter, Indiegogo also supports a wide range of projects, including charitable causes. It offers flexible funding options that allow creators to keep funds raised even if they don't meet their goal.

- *GoFundMe:* The most hit site that categorizes personal causes, medical expenses, and other forms of charitable campaigns.

GoFundMe allows customers to speak about their stories directly and personally to potential donors.

- *Patreon:* Creators and artists can take on Patreon by allowing fans of particular creators to subscribe to various added features in exchange for continual usage. This model ensures an actual community of loyal regular supporters.

- *Fundly:* Fundly is a flexible avenue on which to host your crowdfunding campaigns, be they personal causes or nonprofit initiatives. It offers customization of donation pages and social sharing to widen the reach.

2. Benefits of Crowdfunding Platforms

- *Wider Reach:* Crowdfunding platforms give you access to an audience across the globe; hence, you can present your idea to potential investors other than those in your close circle. This wider reach can bring more visibility and, consequently, more support.

- *Engagement and Community Building:* Most of the crowdfunding options support a lot of communication between creators and backers, generating this community feeling among its patrons in general. Your backer is more inclined towards supporting you.

- *User-Friendly Interface:* The vast majority of crowdfunding sites have user-friendly design and will make navigation extremely effortless at both ends; therefore, it leads to much higher conversion rates.

Among most of the platforms, other tools that come in a package are marketing and promotion. For example, social sharing options and sending email campaigns make it easier to promote your campaign and attract more donors.

Flexibility in Funding Models: Different platforms offer different funding models, such as all-or-nothing and flexible funding. This flexibility lets you choose a model that fits your fundraising goals.

Digital Marketing Strategies

Besides crowdfunding platforms, effective digital marketing strategies are crucial in attracting investors to ensure maximum fundraising. Social media has emerged as one of the most powerful tools for reaching out to potential supporters. Following are some strategies that can be considered:

1. Building a Strong Social Media Presence

- *Choose the Right Platforms:* Determine the right platforms where a target audience would connect. For instance, younger demos may be more active on TikTok and Instagram, but for professional networks, consider LinkedIn.

- *Develop Engaging Content:* Develop a content strategy comprising informative, entertaining, and inspirational posts. Utilize images and videos to get the attention of your audience and put across your message in the most effective way.

- *Success Stories:* Share the impact of your organization's work through success stories and testimonials from beneficiaries. These stories have the potential to touch the hearts of your prospective investors and may lead them to invest in your cause.

2. Utilize Paid Advertising

- **Social Media Ads:** Consider running paid ads on social media to reach a wider audience. Make sure to target based on demographics, interests, and behaviors so that your ads will appear in front of people who would be most interested in your cause.

- **Retargeting Campaigns:** Run retargeting campaigns that reach out to users who have engaged with your content or visited your fundraising page. This could keep your organization top-of-mind and drive potential investors to take action.

3. Engaging with Your Audience

- *Respond to Comments and Messages:* Actively engage with your audience by responding to comments and messages promptly. This interaction fosters a sense of community and shows that you value their input.

- *Live Events:* A good idea would be hosting live events on social media, such as Q&A sessions or virtual fundraisers. This is one great avenue to connect with your audience in real time and to answer questions that they may have about either your organization or fundraising efforts.

4. Influencer Partnerships

- *Identify Relevant Influencers:* Through research, identify those influencers within your space or community whose activities align with the mission of your organization. The collaboration will help you build wider audiences and enhance your credibility.

- *Develop Partnership Opportunities*: Avail opportunities for partnerships that allow the influencer to promote causes to their followers. That may include sponsored posts, events together, or a social media takeover.

5. Measuring and Analysing Results

- Tracking of Engagement Metrics: Make use of analytics to track engagement metrics on your social media platforms. Keep track of likes, shares, comments, click-through rates, and so on to analyze the effectiveness of your content.

- Adjust Strategies by Data: Take this data and refine your digital marketing strategies. Find out what kind of content your audience identifies most with and adjust your approach accordingly. The modern concept of fundraising largely involves the use of technology and platforms.

The crowdfunding platforms provide a very strong avenue for reaching more people and engaging potential investors, while digital marketing strategies-most especially through social media-can increase your voice and attract support to your cause.

Engage in different online methods of raising money, accompanied by equally and appropriately viable digital ways to expose your organization with confidence while building its community that turns support into dollars and cents. Also, remember: Technology has your back if changing the world is really an option that you seek while continuing this fundraising career path.

CHAPTER 12
CULTIVATING A STRONG TEAM

While individual courage and initiative are important, more often than not, the success of your fundraising depends on the overall capabilities of your team. A supportive and coordinated team will help to not only amplify your fundraising endeavors but also strengthen relations with investors and hopefully bottom-line financial support of your mission. This chapter covers how a supportive team could contribute to fundraising and ways to build investor confidence based on the experience and expertise of your team.

The Role of a Supportive Team

A solid team represents the backbone for any type of fundraising campaign. Following are some ways in which a supportive team can build your fundraising capacity:

1. Diverse Skill Sets

A well-rounded team encompasses a diverse array of people with different skills, thus making the process of fundraising smoother and easier. For example:

- *Communications Experts:* Communications-based team members structure engaging stories and elevator pitches to investors of potential opportunities.

- *Data Analysts:* Those individuals capable of running statistical analysis on data develop stories around donor trends and behavior, modifying fundraising strategies when necessary.

- *Marketing Specialists:* The team digital marketing experts help spread the fundraising drive down to the grassroots through social networking and any possible avenue available.

- *Relationship Builders:* Individuals with developed interpersonal skills can develop relationships with donors and stakeholders, fostering continued engagement and support.

2. Collective Problem Solving

Fundraising can be fraught with problems: pressure to meet or exceed ambitious goals, countering donor objections. A team-oriented environment promotes collaboration as team members seek out solutions and ideas from one another. This spirit breeds innovation that has the potential to leverage fundraising efforts.

3. Shared Accountability

When team members work for a common purpose, responsibility lies among the team members. Shared responsibility will keep individuals motivated to work towards the success of the fundraising campaign. Team members can challenge each other on tasks, deadlines, and delivery to ensure everyone is working in the right direction.

4. Better Morale and Motivation

A supportive team environment would maintain morale and motivation at a very high level because when the people within a working team feel appreciated and supported, they are able to show much interest and enthusiasm in their work. Energy may be contagious and drive others to contribute their best in fundraising efforts.

5. Networking

Each member brings in his networks and relationships. Such networks a powerful team could use to expand outreach and connect with investors. By leveraging each member's connection, the team will be able to access an audience that's much wider and increase its chances of securing a financially supporting team.

Demonstrating Expertise and Experience

Aside from the collaborative benefits inherent in a strong team, showcasing expertise and experience in your team can go a long way toward building investor confidence. Here are strategies for effectively highlighting your team's credentials:

1. Create a Compelling Team Profile

Create a profile for the development team that captures qualifications, experiences, and achievements of the different members. This profile can be used throughout the fundraising materials, on your website, and within the presentations to your potential investors. Inclusions should be:

- *Professional Background:* Provide for each member his or her professional history as related to fundraising, nonprofit management, or related fields, including relevant roles and accomplishments.

- *Education and Certifications:* Specify any relevant degree, certification, or training that depicts expertise in areas related to finance, marketing, or program management.

- *Notable Achievements:* Clearly outline the specific achievements that represent how the team performed during past fundraising campaigns or projects. This includes anything from surpassing fundraising goals and landing major donations to successfully launching initiatives.

2. Use Testimonials and Endorsements

Include any testimonials and endorsements from renowned people in your industry or community that speak to the competency and efficiency of your team members. Such recommendations will increase credibility and give confidence to potential investors that they are indeed dealing with a competent and experienced team.

3. Emphasize Team Cooperation

Demonstrate how your team works together to achieve fundraising goals. Share anecdotes or case studies illustrating effective teamwork in action. Emphasizing examples of teamwork where challenges were overcome by team members working together for solutions, or new ideas were developed, helps solidify the notion that your team is not only competent but supportive of each other.

4. Showcase Ongoing Professional Development

Investors are more confident in a team that believes in the concept of continuous professional growth. The training, workshops, and conferences the team members went through for their better grooming should be underlined. The commitment to growth will show your team's intent to stay relevant with new trends and best practices in the industry.

5. Present a United Vision

When highlighting your team, focus on the common vision and mission that hold together members. A unified and focused team about its goals and values can assure investors of their potential. Explain how each team member contributes to the overall mission and how those contribute to driving the organization.

A robust team will help in raising funds and gaining investor confidence. A supportive team gathers people with important skill sets, develops collaboration among them, and maintains a good atmosphere that encourages each of them to excel. Having a good showcase of the experience and expertise of your team provides extra confidence in investors that they are dealing with a capable and committed set of people.

All through your fundraising journey, remember that the power of your team can make all the difference

CHAPTER 13
NAVIGATING LEGAL AND FINANCIAL CONSIDERATIONS

Knowing the legal and financial environment will ensure accountability and engender confidence leading to lasting investor relationships. Such care can protect not just your organization but also your own good reputation and make it credible, even attractive to prospect endorsers. This chapter provides some basic legal requirements one might confront in fundraising and explains a sensible basis of financial disclosure required toward achieving investor confidence.

Understanding Legal Obligations

Fundraising is subject to many different laws and regulations depending on the jurisdiction, and knowledge of these specific legal requirements is necessary. Following are some of the general legal aspects to be considered while fundraising:

1. Registration and Licensing

Most jurisdictions expect organizations to register as charitable organizations before they start soliciting funds. The process for registration often covers:

- A filed exemption will classify most organizations in the United States as 501(c)(3) with the Internal Revenue Service. With that designation, donors can give through tax-deductible contributions that may incentivize giving.

- Other steps include state registration: most states require a separate registration (apart from federal income tax exemption) concerning charitable solicitations. This may require submitting financial statements, bylaws, or such other forms to state authorities.

- Renewal: Several states require annual renewal of charitable registrations, including submission of updated financial reports and confirmation that the organization is in compliance with each state's laws.

2. Compliance with Fundraising Regulations

Organizations must comply with various regulations in conducting fundraising practices. Among the key areas of consideration are:

- *Truth in Advertising:* All communication in fundraising should be honest and not misleading. This relates to describing what donations are for and how they will help.

- *Donor Privacy:* Organizations should respect the privacy and confidentiality of donors. Many jurisdictions have laws around how donor information can be collected, stored, and shared.

- *Gift Acceptance Policies*: Having clear policies about the types of gifts your organization will accept can help minimize legal risks. This includes guidelines on accepting in-kind donations, securities, and other non-cash contributions.

3. Reporting and Accountability

Legal compliance in fundraising has a number of critical components, including transparency and accountability. This includes a requirement for an organization to do the following:

- *Filing of Annual Reports:* Many jurisdictions require nonprofits to file annual reports detailing their financial activities, income, expenses, and programmatic outcomes.

These reports provide a snapshot of the organization's financial health and operational effectiveness.

- **Conduct Audits:** The size and scope of your organization may dictate how big or small financial audits you will be expected to undergo. An audit is a third-party opinion on your financial practices and may help in increasing credibility with donors.

4. Understanding Fundraising Contracts

An organization may enter into contracts in relation to fundraising activities, such as agreements with fundraising consultants or event organizers. It is important to:

- *Review Contracts Carefully:* Ensure that contracts clearly outline the terms of the agreement, including compensation, responsibilities, and deliverables.

- *Seek Legal Counsel:* When in doubt, consult with legal professionals who specialize in nonprofit law to ensure that contracts comply with applicable regulations and protect your organization's interests.

Financial Transparency

Financial transparency is a cornerstone for gaining trust with investors and supporters alike. It goes hand in hand to reassure donors that their contributions are being well used, thus showing accountability. Here is a checklist on key aspects related to financial transparency:

1. Clear Financial Reporting

- *Regular Financial Statements:* Provide regular financial statements on income, balance sheets, and cash flow statements, easily accessible to stakeholders in an understandable format.

- *Budget Transparency:* Your organization's budget, which outlines projected income and expenses, should be shared with your investors. In that way, donors will see where their money falls within the context of overall revenue and how funds will be utilized.

2. Impact Reporting

- *Showing Impact:* Investors need to be shown the outcome of their contributions. Keep them abreast of where the funds are going and what is achieved from such funds. This may include success stories, metrics, and testimonials that show just how well your programs are working.

- *Program-specific reporting:* If your organization runs several programs, consider financial reporting regarding the activities and associated costs for specific programs. This gives donors a greater understanding of how their money makes a difference in specific areas of your work.

3. Open Communication

- *Encourage Questions:* Allow donors to feel comfortable asking questions about the financial practices and reporting of your organization. Open communication helps build trust and further shows the commitment of your organization to transparency.

- *Address Concerns Quickly:* If donors raise questions regarding financial practices or reporting, address these issues as soon as possible and transparently. This responsiveness can help build stronger relationships and improve donor confidence.

4. Utilizing Technology for Transparency

- *Online Financial Portfolios:* Consider placing financial reports, budgets, and impact statements in an online format that donors can access. Accessibility enhances transparency and makes it easier for donors to stay informed.

- *Annual Reports:* Issue an annual report summarizing financial performance, programmatic outcomes of your organization, and any future goals. This same report may be used as an excellent tool in communicating an organization's impact and financial health with various stakeholders.

Knowing how to navigate legal and financial considerations is paramount to successful fundraising. Understanding your legal obligations-including registration, compliance, and reporting requirements-helps to protect your organization and enhances its credibility. In addition, you build trust with investors and supporters through financial transparency. You give clear financial reporting, are able to show your impact, and foster open communications-all ways of assuring potential donors their money will be put to good use.

But as you move along this journey of fundraising, remember: legal and financial considerations are more than what stands in your way; they are opportunities to inspire trust and connections with your supporters.

CHAPTER 14
CELEBRATING SUCCESS AND LEARNING FROM FAILURE

Success often has to be well fought for, and setbacks are all too common. Both success and failure provide great opportunities to learn and to become better. Celebrating milestones promotes morale, as well as a commitment from your team and supporters. On the other hand, reflecting on lessons learned from failure can offer valuable insight into strategy development. This chapter will discuss why milestones in fundraising are so important, and also how looking back at both successes and failures can be used to create an even better next campaign.

Recognizing Milestones

Celebrations of successes along the way build momentum and foster a strong positive organizational culture related to fundraising. Here are many reasons milestones should be acknowledged:

1. Improve morale and motivation

Any accomplishment, no matter how large or small, can significantly raise morale in your team and among its supporters. Such recognition strengthens a sense of accomplishment among those who put in an effort to strive even harder toward the next milestones ahead. Recognizing that hard work and commitment are important and valued often leads to people remaining longer with a given organization, working committedly toward the mission.

2. Building Team Unity

Celebrations afford the opportunity for team members to come together and reflect on their combined efforts. It may be formal events, informal gatherings, or virtual celebrations, but milestone recognitions grease camaraderie and firm up cohesion among the team members. This shared experience can make collaboration and communication smoother for future fundraising processes.

3. Building Relationships with Supporters

It's not just about internal celebration; it extends to your supporters and donors. This may be a good opportunity to express your gratitude and celebrate together the success. This may be through appreciation events, thank-you notes, or even recognizing donors in newsletters or on social media. All these acts of gratitude are ways of solidifying in the minds of your supporters that they are part and parcel of your organization's success.

4. Creating a Culture of Celebration

Building a culture of celebration in your organization inspires a positive attitude and makes the teams resilient. It sets an environment where, after milestones are celebrated, team members will feel free to take risks and pursue bigger goals. This culture can lead to more innovative and creative ways of fundraising.

5. Documenting Achievements

These are ways of keeping a record of achievement and success by celebrating such milestones. Keeping some record of these fundraising milestones, such as attaining a certain financial goal, running a successful campaign, or obtaining a key donor, serves as a reference that can be utilized in the future. This may be through inspiring and motivating your team or even convincing potential investors of your organization's impact.

Reflecting on Lessons Learned

While celebration of successes is critical, it is equally important to reflect on failures and analyze lessons learned. Here are some key strategies for reflecting on successes and failures effectively in order to improve future fundraising efforts.

1. Post-Mortem Evaluations

After any fundraising campaign or effort, do an autopsy to understand what worked and what didn't. Engage your team in this process for multi-dimensional perspectives. Key questions to consider include:

- What were the objectives of the campaign, and were they reached?
- What methods were successful in soliciting donors and gifts?
- What were the challenges we faced, and how did we overcome them?
- What feedback did we receive from donors and supporters?

2. Data Analysis and Metrics

Employ data and metrics in the assessment of effectiveness for your fundraising initiatives. Go through key performance indicators comprising donor retention rates, average gift sizes, and campaign conversion rates. Such quantitative analyses will bring forth areas that need change or improvement, or point out trends for possibly new strategies in the near future.

3. Growth Mindset

Adoption of the growth mindset is one of the most important factors for learning from failures. Not every fall should be perceived as insurmountable stress, but as an impellent to growth and development. Teach your team to embrace a challenge, learn from one's mistakes, and work on perfection. This mindset will inculcate in the team resilience and adaptability needed within the ever-evolving fundraising landscapes.

4. Sharing Lessons with the Team

Build a culture of transparency by sharing what was learned, both successes and failures. Lead the discussion in team meetings or internal communications on what went right and what did not. This open dialogue keeps stimulating their collective learning and puts everyone on the same frequency regarding how to do it in the future.

5. Iteration of Strategies

Use these reflections of past experiences to drive iterations and changes in your fundraising strategy. Sometimes, it's refining the message, shifting the target audience, or using a different channel to reach them-all the learned ability to bend and change can make for even more powerful and effective fundraising.

In every journey of fundraising, there is both success and failure. Celebrating your milestones raises morale and cements the bonds among all parties, besides promoting an element of festivity in the institution. Not to be underemphasized, either, are reflections on the experience from both successes and failures that help draw vital lessons useful in developing future strategies to make it more effective in general.

Every success along the way is cause for celebration, and every failure is a lesson to be learned. In that sense, it's about developing a resilient and motivated team, developing better relationships with supporters, and eventually driving more financial support toward your mission.

CHAPTER 15
THE JOURNEY BEYOND FUNDING

Securing funding marks the beginning of a much bigger process in the journey of fundraising. This is where, after funds are secured, an organization has the very important responsibility to put those funds to work effectively and efficiently in order to accomplish its mission and meet the expectations set forth by the investors. In addition, the journey past funding involves building lasting relationships with investors, cultivating ongoing support and engagement. This chapter will elaborate on what one needs to do after getting funds and how to keep the venture capital investors happy.

What to Do After Securing Funds?

After one successfully secures funding, it is now time to transition from the celebration of excitement to the responsibilities thereafter. Some important steps, among others, include the following:

1. Detailed Implementation Plan

Upon the award of funds, develop a detailed work plan specifying how the funds will be expended. The work plan shall include:

- *Specific Goals and Objectives clearly identified: Clearly* state what you want to accomplish with the grant money: for example, initiating a new program, expanding services, or identifying a particular need in the community.

- *Timeline:* Create a timeline to indicate the roll-out plan for the funded initiatives. This will include key milestones and deadlines, which the management will use to ensure accountability and track progress.

- ***Budget Allocation:*** Describe how the funds will be distributed among various activities, programs, or other needs of operations. Transparency in budget distribution is another vital way of retaining investors' confidence.

2. Investor Communication

After funding, effective communication with investors is very important. Let them know how their money has been spent and the changes it has brought about. Consider the following:

- ***Regular Updates:*** Provide regular updates to the investors regarding progress against goals, challenges experienced, and successes chalked up. This may be in the form of newsletters, emails, or customized reports.

- ***Impact Stories:*** Share dramatic stories of how their contributions are going towards making an impact. Highlight specific beneficiaries or outcomes that show the tangible difference their support is making.

- ***Acknowledgment and Gratitude:*** Let them always know that their support is appreciated. Recognize publically if appropriate, and make them feel valued as a partner in your mission.

3. Monitoring and Evaluation

Establish a system to monitor and evaluate the effectiveness of the various initiatives funded. This includes:

- ***KPI Setting:*** Establish what KPIs would be measurable based on the goals specified. Such indications shall help in assessing the progress and success of the initiatives taken.

- ***Data Collection:*** Regularly collect data to measure the outcomes and impact of the programs through surveys, interviews, or any quantitative metrics indicating trends on outcomes.

- *Strategizing:* Be ready to adjust strategies based on evaluation results. Where some approaches are not working, be dynamic to change to more effective methods.

4. Reporting Back to Investors

Once you have your initiatives in place and have gathered data, you will have to report back to your investors. The areas to cover while reporting include:

- *Financial Accountability:* Account for the money spent to the last coin, for clarity and accountability. This builds trust and your investors feel that their funds are well invested.

- *Impact Assessment*: Share Your Monitoring and Evaluation Results- - Communicate success stories, challenges lessons learned, how their support has been fundamental in moving your mission forward.

Building Lasting Relationships with Investors

Securing funding is just the first step in what should be a long-term relationship with your investors. Building and fostering relationships with them is key to continued support and involvement. Consider the following strategies:

1. Build Thorough Communication

The only way to build trust and rapport with any investor is through open lines of communication. To that end, consider:

- Regular Check-Ins: Schedule regular check-ins with investors to discuss progress, share updates, and address any questions or concerns they may have.

- Personalized Communication: Tailor your communication to each investor's preferences and interests. Some may prefer detailed reports, while others may appreciate brief updates or personal phone calls.

2. Involve Investors in Your Mission

By engaging investors in a mission, the connection with the organization becomes deepened. Some ways to involve them may include:

- *Inviting Participation:* Encourage investors to participate in events, volunteer opportunities, or program activities. Involvement allows for firsthand observation of the impact of their contributions.

- *Seeking Input:* Request their views on the activity or strategies. At this stage in the decision-making process, investors may be brought to a position of ownership and therefore committed to your organization.

3. Celebrate Milestones Together

As highlighted in the previous chapter, milestone celebration is crucial to maintaining excitement and motivation. Invite investors to join these milestone celebrations:

Organize events that showcase successes, or in which their contributions and assistance played a role in realizing such successes from your investors; examples include formal gala parties, informal gatherings, and virtual events.

Share success stories of successes realized with their support during any celebratory remarks. This reiterates the impact of their contributions and further cements their connection to your mission.

4. Create an Avenue for Continuous Engagement

To maintain long-term partnerships, allow the investors an opportunity to stay involved:

- *Advisory Boards:* Establish advisory boards or committees where investors can voice advice and share valuable insights. This will also help them feel more part and parcel of your organization.

- *Exclusive Updates*: Make sure to provide your investors with special updates or insider information regarding the activities that your organization is undertaking. The transparency shall bring forth a feeling of partnership, keeping them interested.

5. Demonstrate Appreciation and Gratitude

Never underestimate the power of gratitude. Let your investors know that their support is valued on a regular basis through things like:

Well-written, personalized thank-you notes after major and minor contributions alike, and upon reaching milestones. A personalized message builds rapport and fosters goodwill.

Add recognition to newsletters, annual reports, or on your website. This ensures public recognition of how important an investor is to an organization.

The post-funding period is a very important stage in the fundraising process. An organization should, after raising funds, ensure implementation in a transparent and accountable way, meeting responsibilities with investors. Long-term relationships with investors are just as critical to continued support and engagement.

By encouraging open communication, bringing investors into your mission, acknowledging milestones, continuing opportunities for investment, and saying thank you, you will be able to build robust, long-lasting relationships that strengthen both your organization and your constituents.

As you continue your fundraising journey, remember it is the relationships you foster and the results you have that will extend far beyond the day the funding is granted.

YOUR REVIEW

Dear Reader,

Let me seize this opportunity to express my deepest gratitude to each and every one of you for sparing your time to read my book, "**EVERY FUNDRAISER:** *Understanding the Courage to Ask and the Factors That Drive Financial Support.*" I am so grateful for your support, and I sincerely hope that the ideas and strategies shared in this book have inspired you in your fundraising activities.

Share Your Thoughts!

If you enjoyed the book, I'd love it if you could take a moment to leave a star review. Your review helps me both as an author to improve, and other readers to find the book. Here's how to leave a review:

1. Head to the store where you bought the book.
2. Find the review section.
3. Rate the book and leave a comment!

Whether it be a few words about what you learned or how the book inspired you, every review counts!

If you enjoyed "**EVERY FUNDRAISER,**" I invite you to explore my other books. Each is crafted with the same passion and dedication to the delivery of insight and useful advice as you have found here. Some of my other works you may want to consider:

- [**THE BOLD & BANKABLE FEMINIST**]
Amazon Book Link: https://www.amazon.com/dp/B0DNTM9QF1

- [**WOMEN'S WORLD OF MONEY**]
Amazon Book Link: https://www.amazon.com/dp/B0DNRC5G5F

- [**THE FINANCIAL ACTIVIST'S BLUEPRINT**]
Amazon Book Link: https://www.amazon.com/dp/B0DNWNRXSC

- [**FROM YOUR SHADOW**]
Amazon Book Link: https://www.amazon.com/dp/B0DP2Z1G2B

- **[THE HIDDEN BATTLE OF GIFTEDNESS]**
Amazon Book Link: https://www.amazon.com/dp/B0DPDN566N

- **[THE INNER WORLD OF CHILDREN]**
Amazon Book Link: https://www.amazon.com/dp/B0DP97Q3LN

- **[LENDING A HELPING HAND]**
Amazon Book Link: https://www.amazon.com/dp/B0DP7DKL17

- **[ESCAPING YOUR HEALTH KILLER]**
Amazon Book Link: https://www.amazon.com/dp/B0DPCGMD8G

You can locate all my books by searching for Olojo Christiana on Amazon with the links above.

Your Support Is Important

Your review and recommendations are of great importance to me in growing my readership, and this will enable me to continue writing. Thank you once again for your support, and I look forward to hearing from you!

Best regards,

Olojo Christiana

ABOUT THE AUTHOR

Olojo Christiana is a passionate advocate for social change and an accomplished fundraising professional with over a decade of experience in the nonprofit sector. With an abiding commitment to empowering communities and driving impactful initiatives, she has dedicated her career to the understanding of fundraising and the psychology behind financial support.

Aside from her on-the-job trainings, Christiana is a noted speaker and workshop facilitator for conferences covering subject matters like fundraising strategies, donor engagement, and the art of the ask. To her, effective fundraising isn't just about bringing in that dollar amount; it is about the relationships that would make someone want to be an integral part of your organization.

Christina is equally committed to the education in fundraising and mentoring. She mentors several fundraisers who are coming along and shares in their journey toward finding ways through what can be an increasingly bewildering environment. Her writings are intended to both inspire the fundraiser and better arm them to do their job.

In "Every Fundraiser: Understanding the Courage to Ask and the Factors That Drive Financial Support," Christiana marshals knowledge and practical experience into an exhaustive guide for all classes of fundraisers. In this, she attempts to break some common myths associated with the concept of fundraising, offers fresh insight into the psychological mechanisms that underline giving, and showcases just how truly rewarding it is to create enduring connections with donors.

Outside of her work and writing, Olojo Christiana enjoys volunteering within her community, seeing new cultures through travel, and spending quality time with her family. She implicitly believes in the power of people coming together to act and in the value of every single person's contribution-a factor that has kept her doing what she does and has inspired many around her.